Communicatio

MW00904493

*Discover The Bes.........yʃ ı0
Communicate
Be Charismatic
Use Body Language
Persuade
& Be A Great Conversationalist*

By Ace McCloud
Copyright © 2014

Disclaimer

The information provided in this book is designed to provide helpful information on the subjects discussed. This book is not meant to be used, nor should it be used, to diagnose or treat any medical condition. For diagnosis or treatment of any medical problem, consult your own physician. The publisher and author are not responsible for any specific health or allergy needs that may require medical supervision and are not liable for any damages or negative consequences from any treatment, action, application or preparation, to any person reading or following the information in this book. Any references included are provided for informational purposes only. Readers should be aware that any websites or links listed in this book may change.

Table of Contents

DEDICATED TO THOSE WHO ARE PLAYING THE GAME OF LIFE TO

KEEP ON PUSHING AND NEVER GIVE UP!

Ace McCloud

Be sure to check out my website for all my Books and Audio books.

www.AcesEbooks.com

Introduction

I want to thank you and congratulate you for buying the book, "Communication Skills: Discover The Best Ways To Communicate, Be Charismatic, Use Body Language, Persuade, And Be A Great Conversationalist."

Communication is the practice of delivering messages between a sender and a receiver. In everyday life, communication is all around us in a variety of different forms. When you get up in the morning and make breakfast for your family, you are communicating to them that you love them and that you want them to have a healthy life. When you walk into your boss' office to talk about the results of the team project, you are communicating that you care about your job. When you raise your arms in an exclamation, you are communicating that you're excited or in shock. When you're driving your car and listening to a radio commercial, a business is communicating to you that they want your business. Those are just a few examples—there are many different ways to communicate, both verbally and non-verbally.

Communication is important for connecting with the masses but more so for connecting with both yourself and the people around you. There is nothing more important that you can do in life than work on mastering your communication skills. If your communication skills are poor, it will likely be very hard to get the results that you want. You will not be able to send a clear message of your wants and expectations to your friends, family, co-workers, clients, or yourself. This often leads to feelings of frustration, confusion, anger and aggravation. Poor communication skills can make it harder for you to advance in your career and assert yourself. You may also find it more difficult to make friends, attract romantic partners, or be close with your family. It may also be challenging to stay positive and optimistic. If you're a businessperson, poor communication skills can make or break your client base and sales.

Finally, having poor communication skills can hinder the image of your true self. You might be a great, friendly, and caring person, but if you're shy and you have a hard time talking to new people or being open, others may perceive you as stuck up or snobby. It will be harder for people to trust and respect you. It can also cause others to perceive you as boring, nervous, weak, or unmotivated. If you're not skilled at communication, you might find yourself without any company and wondering why!

The good news is that mastering your communication skills can eliminate all of those bad possibilities and open the door for endless opportunities. Mastering your ability to communicate can help you become likeable, successful, confident, and powerful. Knowing how to communicate well can help you assert yourself without hurting anyone's feelings. It can take peoples' perception of you from boring to absolutely fascinating! Others will likely perceive you as humorous, truthful, smart and respectable. When you meet new people, your new-found communication skills can help you make friends quicker than ever. If you're a businessperson, knowing how to master your communication skills can help you focus on your audience and boost sales like you've never imagined!

If you want to be truly charismatic with good body language and with the ability to persuade others all while carrying on a pleasant conversation, then communication skills are a must-have! You will likely find that your whole life will improve when you've discovered how to master your ability to get your message across to others. This book contains proven steps and strategies on how to do just that. Best of all, anybody can improve and master their communication skills! It doesn't take a college degree or an inborn talent. All you need is a little bit of knowledge, insight, and action. This book will give you the knowledge and insight. If you want that extra boost to take massive action and get things done then be sure to check out my Self Discipline and Motivation Books!

In just a few short pages, you will discover the in's and out's of mastering your communication skills. In Chapter 1, you will learn about the communication process and how to identify your own communication style so that you know where to start and where to set your end goal. In Chapter 2, you will discover the secrets that will help you become more charming and charismatic so that you come off as more likeable. In Chapter 3, you will learn how to pair body language with verbal communication and how to use it together to your advantage. Chapter 4 holds the key to improving your persuasion skills so that you can get the results that you want. Finally, Chapter 5 will explore the different things you can do to become an engaging conversationalist, a must-read for those who have difficulty talking to others or striking up conversations.

Chapter 1: The Best Ways to Communicate

Communication is powerful. Kingdoms and wars have been won and lost based on effective communication. The basic definition of communication is when a message travels from a sender to a receiver. If you are telling your spouse about your day, you are sending a message and your spouse is the receiver. If you are watching TV and you suddenly stumble upon a commercial for Burger King, who is trying to sell you a Whopper, you are the receiver and Burger King is the sender. There are many ways to communicate—through talking, television, radio, or even visual advertisements. Sometimes the receiver is unable to receive the full message. This is usually called noise or communication barriers.

A communication barrier is something that prevents the receiver from understanding the message that a sender is sending. Communication barriers are common because there are many different types of communication. There are physical barriers, which means that something is physically preventing you from receiving a message. This could be anything from a large distance between you and the sender or something like a closed door or a bad signal. Then there are internal barriers. These types of barriers are internal influences, such as racism or bias. Emotional barriers are another common type. If you are feeling strong emotions, such as fear or anxiety, it can prevent you from fully receiving a message. If you are receiving a message from someone who does not share your language or culture, then you may experience a language/cultural barrier. Finally, there are gender barriers and intrapersonal barriers. In the event of a gender barrier, you may not understand something because of your gender. Shyness is a common intrapersonal barrier.

Types of Communication

There are two main types of communication: **verbal** and **non-verbal.** Verbal communication is when you use words, either written or orally, to convey a message to your audience. Non-verbal communication is when you send a message without using words. This usually consists of using body language to get across a message to your audience. There are 3 sub-categories of both types of communication: **intrapersonal, interpersonal**, and **mass** communication. Intrapersonal communication is when you communicate with yourself. Interpersonal communication is when you communicate with others. Mass communication is when you communicate with a large group of people.

There are also some other types of communication that derive from these two categories. **Written** communication is verbal communication that utilizes written words. Reading the daily newspaper is a good example of written communication. **Oral** communication is verbal communication that utilizes spoken words. When you give a presentation in front of a group of people, that is oral communication. **Formal** communication is a type of communication that utilizes official rules. When you write messages that have good sentence structure and correct grammar, you are using formal communication. Finally, there is **informal** communication. Informal communication is when you don't follow an official set of rules. For example, if you talk in slang, you are using informal communication.

Styles of Communication

Now that you understand how communication works and what can get in the way of it, it is time to learn about the main styles of communication. Your style of communication can reflect a lot about yourself and influence how successful you are in life. By better understanding these styles and figuring out which style describes you, you can determine if you need to change your style or work on improving it.

Assertive. An assertive communication style often equates to your self-confidence. Not many people are able to achieve this style, so if you can do it, it can really make you stand out. People who exhibit this style of communication tend to be high achievers or leaders. They are generally secure and can easily express themselves. They tend to be decisive, responsible, and accepting of failure. In terms of non-verbal communication, assertive people tend to have a medium-toned voice, a relaxed posture, and the ability to make good eye contact. The best benefit of being an assertive communicator is that other people are more likely to trust you. An assertive communication style is the best one to have. Check out this YouTube video by RealTrainingRightNow, Being Assertive, to learn about some great ways to help yourself achieve this style of communication.

Aggressive. People who are aggressive communicators are often loud, more prone to be violent and can be sarcastic. Aggressive communicators tend to act as bullies and can come off as very demanding. They tend to be loud-toned, irritated, invasive and unhappy. Aggressive communicators don't tend to smile and they often come off as "bigger than you." When you are an aggressive communicator, people can act defensive towards you. To see some examples of aggressive communication and behavior, check out this helpful YouTube video by expertvillage: Examples of Aggressive Body Language.

Passive-Aggressive. People who are passive-aggressive communicators often appear calm on the outside but tend to be aggressively indirect in their communication. They often feel that they are powerless. Therefore, they tend to be vengeful in spirit. The most common habits of passive-aggressive communicators include being indirect, sulky and complaining a lot. In terms of non-verbal communication, these types of people tend to talk with a sweet voice. They often keep their arms crossed or place their hands on their hips. They usually display innocent facial expressions and often appear warm and friendly. However, receivers will usually end up confused, angry, or hurt by these types of communicators. There are some good tips on How To Confront Passive Aggressive Behavior in this YouTube video posted by About.com.

Submissive. People who are submissive communicators often feel that they have to please others. Submissive communicators are more likely to let people trample on them just to avoid conflict. They often feel that their opinions don't matter. Submissive communicators often tend to be apologetic, lazy, indecisive, unmotivated, soft-spoken and "small." They often fidget and never attempt to make eye contact. Receivers may take advantage of these types of communicators or end up frustrated with them.

Manipulative. Those who have a manipulative communication style are usually good at controlling people. They come off as good influencers but their true intentions are to use people. Manipulative communicators tend to be shrewd, insincere and envious. They often use their emotions to guilt people into doing what they want. Their posture and facial expressions change a lot and their voices tend to be high-pitched. Receivers will often feel guilty, annoyed and resentful. Check out this YouTube video posted by eHow to see some of the most common signs of manipulation, Communication & Understanding Others: Signs of Manipulation. The video is centered around relationships, but you can apply the signs to almost any situation.

Overcoming Communication Barriers

Listening is a form of communication that is often forgotten. However, it is a powerful method and can often break down most barriers. Listening is the most important part of communication. Listening helps your brain process the words that you are hearing. It is an integral part of effective and efficient communication. Bad listeners tend to think faster than they can talk. Most significantly, listening is a sign of sincerity—it shows the other person that you care and you are truly interested in what they have to say. It is important to develop your listening skills because they can create connections and dissolve barriers. Listening relieves tension and can help instill confidence in both parties. This section will provide you with some great tips on how to boost your listening skills.

Avoid Distractions. Distractions are detrimental to good listening skills. If you're not solely focused on the other person who is communicating with you, it will be hard to really process what they're saying. Phones and electronics are the worst types of distractions. Put away anything that might distract you when talking to someone else and if possible, communicate in an area that has minimal distractions. I can't tell you how many fights and arguments have erupted over the last twenty because someone was focusing on something else besides the person who was trying to communicate with them. People like to be valued. If they perceive that you value other things, especially an inanimate object, over them, they tend to get highly upset if they have a good self-esteem! People will have much more respect for you if you ignore that phone call or instant message and instead keep your full attention on them!

Utilize All Senses. When listening to someone else speak, take advantage of touch, sight, sound, and even smell. You can use your other senses to heighten your listening experience, which may also help you focus better.

Respond When Appropriate. This point speaks for itself. If someone is talking to you and they stop to ask you a question and you don't respond either verbally or non-verbally, they will know right away whether or not you are listening to them.

Don't Interrupt. If you interrupt the person who is talking, it will show right away that you're not actively listening. Wait for a pause or break in the conversation where you can chime in. Also try not to shift the conversation unless it is appropriate.

Check out this fun YouTube video by The Professional Training Academy, <u>Test Your Listening Skills</u>, to put your newly developed listening skills to the test. If you get all the questions right, you've probably mastered your listening skills well! If you miss a few of the answers or don't do a very good job, it may be a sign to practice working on your listening skills.

Chapter 2: Discover How To Be Charming and Charismatic

Knowing how to be charming and charismatic is important for being a good communicator. To be charismatic is to be likeable despite your physical appearance. Many people are under the misconception that you have to have a striking physical appearance to be likeable and convincing, but the truth is that all you need is charisma. Some of the most charismatic people in the world and throughout history have been average looking at best. Maybe because they actually had to work at it! The better you are at being charming and charismatic, the more likely you will be able to influence people and get through to them. All it takes is learning how to develop your charisma and put it into practice. This chapter will help you discover how you can become charming and charismatic yourself.

The most important part of being charismatic this way is to establish a sense of honesty and trust about yourself. Lying in any context is ineffective to being a great communicator. It often gets you nowhere and it usually comes back to haunt you in the future. People generally lie to avoid conflicts or to get out of taking responsibility. However, lying becomes a major communication barrier and many people are skilled at knowing whether or not you are being truthful. It is also difficult to recover your reputation once you have been labeled as dishonest.

The key to being charming and charismatic is to be diplomatic. Your goal is to send your message without offending the receiver. Being truthful is the first step to becoming charming and charismatic. Once you have mastered that ability, and the ability to relay information in a pleasant and effective manner, then you are well on your way to becoming charismatic, especially if you practice and really try!

Be Self-Confident. Without self-confidence, it is going to be very hard to come off as charming and charismatic. You have to like yourself before others can like you. You have to have a positive, optimistic outlook on life. If you are not comfortable with yourself, it will be hard to stay confident and positive. If you're not positive, it will be harder to get people to want to be around you.

Throw Body Language into the Mix. When you are responsive to the things happening around you, it usually makes you much more likeable. Think of it this way—if you see your aunt for the first time in 10 years and she starts throwing her arms up and smiling when she sees you, you are likely going to feel loved, special, excited, etc. But if she sees you for the first time in 10 years and doesn't have any type of reaction, you will likely be inclined to feel awkward or confused. Using body language and gestures to respond to the things happening around you often lightens up the mood for everybody and it helps eliminate tension. It's also a great way to practice extroversion. Be sure to keep an eye out for your favorite body language movements from your friends, family, celebrities, etc. and then practice using them for yourself!

Master a Contagious Laugh. <u>Laughter</u> and smiling is great for easing tension and becoming open to others, but only if done in a real way. The good news is that a genuine smile is usually a byproduct of a genuine laugh. You can also practice smiling, which has been proven to increase your mood and reduce depression! However, it is your laugh that you want to pay attention too. Next time you laugh, be aware. Is it a contagious laugh? Is it an obnoxious laugh? Is it a forced laugh? Is it a haughty and superior laugh? Pay attention to your laugh and try to work on getting it to be contagious and genuine. This is likely to make you appealing and memorable.

Be a Social Toucher. When you lightly touch someone on their back or shoulder, it instantly creates a warm connection between you and that person. It helps you come off as friendly and inviting. With this strategy, it is important to use good judgment. Do not do anything that may come off as sexual harassment or unwanted touching.

Don't Wear a Poker Face. Your face is a powerful slate. Many people can pick up messages by the expression on your face. If you wear a poker face it may be hard to read and you and may come off as closed and cold. Try not to wear your hair or bangs over your forehead, because that is the most important part of your face for being expressive.

Be Open With Strangers. It may be hard, especially for introverts, but when you are open and outgoing with those who you don't know, it can make you very likeable. Interestingly, research shows that introverts like to be around extroverts and vice versa. Put the genuine communication skills that you learn in this book to use when engaging in conversation with strangers and you will get the valuable practice and reactions that make life fun!

Be A Story Teller. People who have great stories to tell often leave an impressionable footprint in the lives of others. Do cool, amazing things so that you can speak about it later. Talk with confidence and relevance. Add humor when appropriate. Just be careful when you tell your story. If you do it right after someone else, they may feel like you are trying to outdo them and become offended.

Talk About The Other Person. When talking to people, focus on them. If they are a person who is all about boats, find a way to integrate boats into the conversation. This helps build rapport and it establishes a sense of trust, respect, and likeability. The other person will likely feel comfortable with you instantly. Look for areas of similarity and be sure to talk about them. It is always enjoyable to talk about things that both people find interesting.

Practice Good Listening. As we talked about earlier, it is always, be an active listener. This definitely bears repeating! If there is one thing you take from this book, it is that good listening skills are critical in so many ways in communication and in life! Pay attention, use gestures to show you hear them, and engage in the conversation. No matter what kind of communication you are involved in, active listening is always a "must."

Here are some more great YouTube videos that you can watch to get a better idea about how to master your charm and charisma:

Charisma Breakdown – Tony Robbins' Body Language by Charisma on Command

Charisma Breakdown – Bill Clinton Eye Contact by Charisma on Command

Charming People With Your Voice by Brian Tracy

Chapter 3: The Best Ways To Use Body Language

Body language is a form of non-verbal communication, meaning that gestures replace spoken words. Body language often complements verbal communication by reinforcing the message that you are trying to send. Body language can be subtle or non-subtle and includes everything from the way you walk, stand, sit, and move to the expression on your face. Understanding how to use body language can greatly strengthen your ability to communicate with others. It can also help you better understand others who are trying to communicate with you. Understanding how to properly use body language with verbal communication is important because if used improperly, it can create confusion and mistrust.

Non-Verbal Cues Explained

Body language and other non-verbal cues can be broken down into 5 categories. These categories show how non-verbal cues work with verbal communication to become powerful. You can use this knowledge to better understand how body language works.

Accenting occurs when a non-verbal cue emphasizes a verbally spoken message. For example, if somebody is clearly expressing anger and they start walking forward with their finger pointed at you, that is accenting. You can tell from that combination that the person who is angry really wants you to get the point. Check out this YouTube video by Barron Cruz, <u>Demonstrating non-verbal accenting</u>, to see an example of accenting.

Substitution occurs when somebody makes a gesture in place of a verbal message. For example, if you were at a party with someone and they nodded their head toward the door with a desperate facial expression, you would probably figure out that they want to leave.

Repetition occurs when your body language aligns with your verbal message. For example, Homer Simpson buys a transportation device in Treehouse of Horror VIII. When his son Bart asks to use it, Homer tells him how dangerous it can be and he yells "Kablamo!" while extending his arms out to signify a big explosion. Homer was using arm gestures to emphasize his point about the danger of his transportation device.

Contradiction occurs when your body language disagrees with your verbally spoken message. For example, if you are nervously rubbing your eyes while saying, "It wasn't me", the person you are talking to will likely figure out that you are lying.

Complementing occurs when your gestures go along with your verbally spoken message. For example, if you're delivering bad news, you may hang your head low and speak in a sad voice.

Common Types of Body Language

Body language can be any type of movement or gesture, but here are the most common ones that have the most impact on communication:

- Posture
- Hand gestures
- Facial expressions
- Touch
- Eye contact
- Voice tone/pace/volume
- Space and distance

For an amazing explanation of all body language and gestures, I highly recommend taking a few minutes to check out this YouTube video by Derek Banas: <u>Gestures and Body Language Tutorial</u>.

<u>Confident</u> people tend to have a tall posture, solid eye contact, a moderate voice, and slow, clear speech. They are well experienced in using hand gestures to communicate. Body language is especially important for building rapport with other people. The more rapport you can build between you and another person, the more likeable you will be to them and the more leverage you will have in your relationship.

Here are some great tips for using body language to build rapport:

Mimic Body Language. A little into your conversation, notice the body language of both you and the person you're talking with. Are you both sitting the same way? Are you both relaxed and sunk into your chair or is one of you learning forward with your elbows on your arms? When you've matched the body language of your partner, you're both in rapport. This is a tactic the best in the world use all the time! This also applies to in many other ways. If the other person likes to talk loudly, you can mirror this and talk loudly. The other person will more than likely be more inclined to like you, because you are like them.

Don't Be Tense or Stiff. Other people will instantly be able to pick up if you're tense, stiff, or otherwise feeling awkward. If you're feeling that way, it is likely that you will make the other person feel that way too.

Use Eye Contact. As always, be sure to make eye contact with those you are speaking with. This will help capture their attention and they will know that you're listening intently. This is very important, especially if you are trying to impress the opposite sex.

Stand Straight. If you're standing during your conversation, sit up straight. This will promote confidence in both yourself and the person who you are talking with.

Control Your Smile. Smiling is important for coming off as warm and friendly but don't smile for too long. Otherwise, it may give your audience the wrong impression and make them feel uncomfortable.

Respond When Appropriate. When the time is right, respond to the person you are talking with. Nod, reply, smile, or give off some other gesture to let them know that you're listening and engaged.

How to Read Body Language

When it comes to being an expert on reading body language, there are a few important things you should know. First, it is important not to read too much into one cue or gesture—instead, look at them all as a whole. Think back to the different types of cues and how they work with verbal communication. Second, it is important to look for inconsistencies. Always make sure that your or another person's verbal and nonverbal communications match. Finally, always go with your gut feelings. If you have a gut feeling about how somebody is using body language to communicate with you, you are probably correct.

Chapter 4: How To Be Persuasive And Get What You Want

Persuasion is a powerful technique in which you can convince other people to see things from another angle, which is most often your point of view. Many people who work in the field of marketing are good at persuasion. Persuasion is a very useful skill to have when you're pitching a sale, marketing, or making a speech. Most importantly, learning persuasion skills can help you become a very powerful person. Not many people are good at persuasion, so if you can master it, you can be one step ahead of the game. If you can persuade others, more people will be likely to respect you. The strength of your communication skills often defines the strength of your persuasion skills. The most powerful people in history have mastered this skill!

Persuasion Tips

Know Your Audience. **Without knowing anything about your audience, it will be really hard to be persuasive.** If you're making a speech or a sales pitch, it is important to research your audience beforehand so you know how to get into their heads. Another tip is to learn how to build rapport. Match the body language of your audience and talk to them in a way in which they can understand. For example, if you're talking to a bunch of engineers, go ahead and use engineering jargon.

Don't Be Manipulative. Know the difference between persuasion and manipulation. Manipulation is when you forcefully coerce others into doing something that you want or try and trick them with misleading or false information. The best use of persuasion is when others do something voluntarily, that is in their best interest, and it also benefits you at the same time.

Pay Attention to Context and Timing. You can often create a set of standards that you can use from these two factors. In many areas of life, timing is everything! If you can frame something in the right context at the right time, then your chances of success in persuasion increase dramatically!

Talk To People About Themselves. Make your audience the center of your conversation. By doing this, you can get them to become more interested in what you're saying and you will have their attention for a longer period of time. Don't focus on yourself but your audience. You can also learn more about them and search for areas of common interest that you may both enjoy talking about.

Use Reciprocity to Your Advantage. It is human nature to do something for a person who has done something nice for you. See if you can somehow slip in a favor or good deed when trying to be persuasive. More likely than not, your audience will want to return the favor.

Be Persistent. People like to see when others go after what they want and continue to prove their value even after a failed attempt or two. Never give up and be persistent in your efforts. Don't be too pushy or overbearing but don't give up after the first failure. Use any failure to learn from your mistakes and switch up your strategy until you've found success. There are hundreds of stories of the beautiful maiden won by the average man who would just never give up, and thousands of stories of great men, like Abraham Lincoln, who faced adversity after adversity but who persevered through it all to incredible success!

Give Sincere Compliments. Handing out a genuine compliment can help build trust and respect. When done strategically, it can really help you win over your audience. Only give out sincere compliments and don't overdo it. Give out enough to help your audience understand that they are in your best interest.

Set Expectations For Yourself. When it comes to persuasion, you must be truthful and you must mean what you say. If you're trying to persuade your audience to make an investment, you will have to prove to them that you can deliver on what you're saying. Have some examples of past successes to point to. When your audience knows that you can deliver on your promises, they are more likely to trust you and take action.

Never Assume. Never assume the needs of your audience. Instead, focus on purely delivering value. Common assumptions are usually about money, time, and other limited resources. However, don't be afraid to put yourself out there and take risks. Never assume that your audience doesn't have money or that they wouldn't be interested.

Use Scarcity and Urgency To Your Advantage. When people know there is only a limited amount of something, the chances of them wanting it go up. It's a general, classic marketing technique. Be sure to make your audience understand that what you are offering them is scarce. This will likely make them jump to take action. Add in some urgency, which will motivate your audience. If they are not motivated right away to take action, their chances of doing it can highly decrease. That is why the limited edition collectibles are worth so much over time!

Use Visuals. Visuals are a powerful marketing technique and can really help you persuade your audience. Use a visual when you first meet your audience so that you can create a memorable, lasting impression. Then see if there are any other ways to use visuals to your advantage. For example, if you're trying to get your audience to invest into a cruise line, you could use pictures of people relaxing on a Hawaiian beach to get them excited. In this day in age, there is so much visual pictures out there that it can be very inexpensive to portray a professional yet inexpensive image.

Use Behavior to Your Advantage. Humans have many different persuasive behaviors that lead others to take action. Think about when a child cries because it wants an ice cream sundae. The child is likely trying to get its parent to say yes.

That being said, you shouldn't act like a child when it comes to persuading your audience. However, you can work different behaviors into your sales pitch to try and get your foot in the door.

Be Energetic. When talking to your audience, be as energetic as possible. Use a combination of verbal communication, body language and non-verbal cues. Move around, interact with your audience and engage them. If you come off as boring, your audience may very well fall asleep on you or tune you out. I can't tell you how many boring teachers I had in my educational experience, but the energetic and positive ones always stand out even years later! Try to keep the energy flowing to keep your audience listening.

Being Persuasive=Being Confident

Most importantly, you must be confident if you want to successfully persuade others. Humans have a solid ability to see right through you and they can often tell whether you are confident or scared out of your mind. Since people are likely to judge you this way, it is important to be as confident as possible when communicating with your audience. This section will provide you with some great, easy tips to look and feel confident.

Keep Your Hands Out Of Your Pockets. Some people have a nervous habit of keeping their hands in their pockets when interacting with their audience. Doing this can reflect nervousness, make you look uncomfortable and it promotes bad posture.

Don't Fidget. Fidgeting is another common nervous habit to avoid at all costs. Fidgeting also reflects nervousness as well as insecurity and boredom. A good way to prevent yourself from fidgeting is to keep your hands on a flat surface.

Stand Up Straight. Standing up straight is a great way to come off as confident. It reflects inner strength and also discourages insecure walking. A good way to promote straight posture is to train your abs, lower back, and glute muscles.

Perfect Your Personal Appearance. From head to toe, it is important to practice perfecting your personal appearance. The way you dress, keep your hair, and even the way you smell can have a lasting effect on others. Always keep yourself clean and well-groomed.

Develop a Firm Handshake. Having a firm handshake reflects confidence and it gives off a feeling of enthusiasm and warmth. Try not to cut off a handshake too short and shake the fingers, never a good way to win bonus points.

NLP Techniques

Finally, another way to practice your persuasion skills is to learn some NLP techniques. NLP is a process that uses components of modern psychology to build rapport among people and help change perceptions. NLP promotes both personal and interpersonal relations.

NLP Technique #1: Association and Disassociation

Learning this technique can help you influence others to associate you with positive images and feelings. This technique is very easy to do and the more effective your communication skills are, the more effective this technique will be. To use this technique, only talk about positive things when talking to other people. Work your friends into the conversation and don't talk about yourself too much. This will help people begin to associate you with positivity, thus making you more likeable. Avoid negativity and others will be more inclined to like you.

NLP Technique # 2: Building Rapport

Building rapport is key to building strong interpersonal connections with others. Practicing this technique can help you learn how to adapt to different situations. You already know some ways to build rapport from the other chapters of this book. When talking with another person, be aware of any keywords and speaking patterns that you can pick up on and match. Try to match everything down to the breathing rate of the other person. Acknowledge the other person's interests and do not focus on yourself. Learning this powerful technique can help you become very successful in all areas of life.

NLP Technique #3: Model Success

This technique is the process of analyzing the behaviors of others so that you can emulate their patterns. Find somebody who is successful and treat them as your model. The beauty of this technique is that it helps you avoid experimenting with your behavior. You can find somebody who is already successful and jump right into success. Modeling after somebody doesn't steal your identity. Rather, it helps instill solid habits into your lifestyle. Once you have picked your role model, watch how they behave. Research their actions, thoughts, and feelings. Once you've done that, you can imitate and emulate. A good strategy is to pick somebody who has mastered something you haven't. For example, if you're trying to be more charismatic, find a charismatic role model. This is way better and more productive than trying to figure out everything on your own when a bit of research could have saved you hundreds of hours of time and effort!

Body Language and Persuasion

Finally, you can take what you've learned about using body language and implement it into your persuasion strategy. How you present yourself can have a huge impact on how persuasive you are. There are three key non-verbal cues you can implement into your communication style to top off your ability to persuade.

First, always stand tall, because it shows confidence. Second, practice your ability to speak in a lower tone of voice. Third, think of powerful memories that made you feel confident in the past. Thinking of those memories can motivate and inspire you to go after the results you want. For example, one of my favorite memories was when I was a senior in high school at the state championship track meet. It was the last race of the day, and the winner would determine who won the state championships! It was the 4 by 400 meter relay race. My team was ranked in lane 8, the worst lane to be in. I was second to run. The race started well with my teammate off to a good start. However, after the first 300 meters he lost steam and people started to pass by him. I was sitting at the relay line in sort of shock. It seemed like slow motion. I finally got the baton while literally standing still and just begging him to get there! He was in last place when I got the baton. I took off as fast as I could, the crowd right next to my shoulder as I was in the outer lane. I was making up ground, but when it came time to merge into the first lanes I got cut off and was forced to hold the last position. As we came around the last turn I had a huge surge of motivation and I remember thinking "This is the last race of my high school career!" I kicked it into overdrive and passed four people as I gave off the baton in what was the fastest I had ever run the 400m in my life! Our true hero of the team was the recipient of the hand off. He was the state champion 100m and 200m runner and it was amazing to watch his six foot plus body just run to the first position and hold it all the way through to the next handoff. I wish I had this recorded, but I remember it clear as day. Our team was screaming and going wild! We had the final leg in first place with a solid runner, the second best on our team. But the team that could beat us for the state championships had a great distance runner, and he passed us. Then after two hundred meters our guy passed him. Then the other team passed us again, then, one last time, our guy passed him and went on to win the race and the state championships! I was the captain of that team and the most beautiful girl on our women's team ran over and gave me a big hug! So whenever I need some extra motivation, I will think of that! Be sure to remember your own great victories and record them and view them often, they are great motivation boosters!

More Great Resources on Persuasion

Speech Writing: How To Write a Great Persuasive Speech

Check out these persuasive commercials to get a good idea of what you can emulate– Notice how the actor in the commercial tries to be just like you and also notice how they talk directly to you, the consumer. Most of these commercials tell you all the benefits of each product and what it can do for you, usually focusing on "ease." Most of them capitalize on beauty, fashion, health, exercise, performance, and food, all of which most people hold in high regard.

Chapter 5: How To Be A Great Conversationalist

Having solid communications skills is important for being able to carry on interesting and memorable conversations. Conversations make up the majority of your daily communication, so it is important to know how to master them. After all, if you're not good at talking to people, it can close many doors of opportunity for you. To be an engaging conversationalist, the first thing you should do is refer back to the different types of communication styles in Chapter 1. Engaging in a conversation can be difficult for some, especially if you are shy and in a new situation. However, you can use the tips in this chapter to help you overcome your fear of talking to new people. At the end of this chapter, you will find a section of conversation starters that you can use next time you find yourself in that situation.

Be Direct and Assertive. If you try to beat around the bush or hint at things, you probably will not get very far, which can leave both parties confused and frustrated. Just say how you feel or what you want in a polite, respectful way. Especially when dealing with significant others. It is better to be blunt than deal with all the other issues that can come when expectations are not met!

Be Confident. Without self-confidence, it is often very hard to hold an engaging conversation. If you don't think highly of yourself, you will usually assume that others think of you that way to and it can be challenging to hold engaging conversations. Walk into each conversation with a confident mindset. Notice the differences when you do.

Say Hi First. Believe it or not, many people are shy, so if you just go ahead and say hi to someone first, 9 times out of 10 they will begin to have a conversation with you. Don't forget to wear a warm, inviting smile on your face. Once again, feel free to practice smiling on your own. Not only will it help you in genuine situations, it is a great way to improve your mood!

Practice Good Eye Contact. I'll mention this again. Look at your partner's eyes when speaking. This shows that you're actively listening and that you are genuinely engaged in the conversation. The most powerful and charismatic people in the world are pros at good eye contact!

Be Funny When Called For. Sometimes being humorous can break any tension during a conversation. It's also a great way to become likeable. Don't try to be funny all the time, though, and only inject it when the time is appropriate.

Start Conversations About News or a Trending Topic. If you're not sure how to start a conversation, talk about something that most people are bound to know about. This is usually a current news story or a trending topic. Once you each begin to start talking to each other, you can get to know each other more and look out for cues on where to take the conversation.

Smile Genuinely. There is nothing more friendly and inviting then a warm smile. If you see somebody who is not smiling, chances are you will question whether you should approach that person or not. A smile can make you seen open and up for a conversation.

Read Avidly. During your free time, read as much as you can. This way, you can pick up all sorts of knowledge, which can make great conversation topics in the future. This also makes you more versatile, so you're more likely to have something to talk about with everyone.

Don't Act Hostile. Don't act hostile, intimidating, or in any other manner that might make others feel inferior.

Use Names. If you've just met somebody, find out their name and use it throughout your conversation. If it's somebody you know, start the conversation by saying their name. This makes it much more personal.

Act Natural. When speaking to someone, act natural. If you are uncomfortable speaking or tense, your partner will often be able to sense this and then the conversation risks becoming awkward.

Avoid Speaking Passively. Speak actively and avoid using a passive voice. Those who speak actively tend to be much more interesting and engaging. It also makes the conversation easier to understand.

Speak Truthfully. Only talk about things that you can truthfully discuss. Don't be a hypocrite and don't change your opinion just to match others.

Don't Fill Silence. Sometimes a short period of silence in a conversation can be a good thing. Don't try to fill up gaps with conversation. That can sometimes create an awkward situation and it may give off a vibe to others that you talk too much.

Don't Mumble. Don't mumble or use words such as "like" or "um." When you eliminate these from your conversation, it often flows much nicer and you are usually easier to understand.

Avoid Profanity. When having a conversation, try to avoid using profanity, especially if you're speaking in a professional manner. Be aware of your audience or partner and avoid using any other words or phrases that may come off as inappropriate or offensive.

Be Aware of Your Voice. When you talk to others, take note of the tone, volume, and pitch of your voice. If you speak too softly, it may be difficult for others to hear you. On the other hand, if you speak too loudly, it may be difficult for others to listen to you. Try to come up with a medium speaking style that fits well in most speaking situations.

Breathe. Finally, don't forget to breathe! If you're nervous, sometimes it is only natural to hold your breath without realizing it. Allow yourself to relax and don't get too stressed out.

Some Awesome Conversation Starters

Where did you get that _____? It's really nice!

What do you think about _____?

It must be _____ to have a _____!

What made you _____?

Why do you think your company is _____?

How do you know _____?

What type of phone do you have?

If you could meet anyone in history, who would you pick?

Do you exercise? How often?

Do you play sports or have a favorite sports team?

Where in the world have you traveled?

What is your favorite movie/actor?

What is your favorite book/author?

What is your favorite type of music to listen to?

Who is your role model?

Where do you see yourself in 5 years?

What is your biggest fear?

What is the best piece of advice you've ever heard?

What is the craziest thing you've ever done?

Are you a coffee drinker?

Do you speak any other language?

These are just a few basic starters but they are open-ended enough to help you spark up a really great conversation. Don't limit yourself to these, though. Be willing to ask other people questions that may be appropriate in your context.

Conclusion

You now know how important it is to have great communication skills! Remember, communication is a process. The two main types are verbal and non-verbal, verbal dealing with words and non-verbal dealing with movements and gestures. There are many different kinds of communication barriers, but mastering it can help you easily conquer them! Also, don't forget just how important the skill of listening is.

Keep in mind the different styles of communication. It is my hope that you've figured out which one's that fit you best and if it's not "assertive," I hope that you make it a goal to get there. With the great communication skills that you have just read about, you now have the ability to persuade other people and be an engaging conversationalist despite your level of confidence or shyness.

I hope this book was able to help you to bring everything together communication and give you some great ideas on what you can use and practice on. Moreover, I hope you were able to learn some new things in an efficient and time-effective manner.

The next step is to start doing some great things in your life with your newly acquired knowledge. What do you need to work on in terms of your own communication skills? Do you have a big speech coming up? Is there someone you want to be closer with? Focus on Chapter 4 and really put your persuasion skills to the test! Do you need to work on moving from submissive to assertive? Refer back to Chapter 2 and start being more aware of how you communicate with those around you. You might need to work on all of your communication skills or just some. However, you may only need to work on a few areas. Write down 3 to 5 goals that you want to achieve in terms of communication, go out there, and get your results!

Finally, if you discovered at least one thing that has helped you or that you think would be beneficial to someone else, be sure to take a few seconds to easily post a quick positive review. As an author, your positive feedback is desperately needed. Your highly valuable five star reviews are like a river of golden joy flowing through a sunny forest of mighty trees and beautiful flowers! *To do your good deed in making the world a better place by helping others with your valuable insight, just leave a nice review.*

My Other Books and Audio Books
www.AcesEbooks.com

Business & Finance Books

LEADERSHIP

THE TOP 100 BEST WAYS
TO BE A GREAT LEADER

Ace McCloud

MARKETING

*The Top 100 Best Things That You
Can Do In Order To Make Money &
Be Successful With Marketing*

Ace McCloud

FACEBOOK

THE TOP 100 BEST WAYS
TO USE FACEBOOK FOR BUSINESS,
MARKETING & MAKING MONEY

Ace McCloud

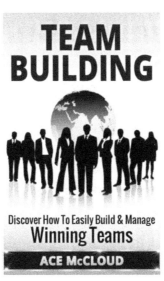

**TEAM
BUILDING**

Discover How To Easily Build & Manage
Winning Teams

ACE McCLOUD

MONEY

THE TOP 100 BEST WAYS
TO MAKE AND MANAGE MONEY

Ace McCloud

TWITTER

HOW TO MARKET & MAKE
MONEY WITH TWITTER

Ace McCloud

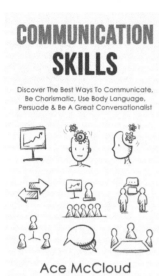

Peak Performance Books

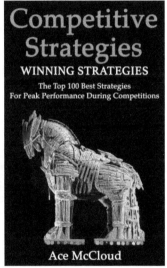

Be sure to check out my audio books as well!

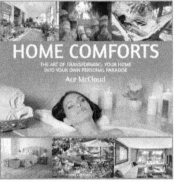

Check out my website at: **www.AcesEbooks.com** for a complete list of all of my books and high quality audio books. I enjoy bringing you the best knowledge in the world and wish you the best in using this information to make your journey through life better and more enjoyable! **Best of luck to you!**

CPSIA information can be obtained
at www.ICGtesting.com
Printed in the USA
LVHW101602300620
659399LV00007B/366